I CAN LIVE

Living Through Crisis

Andrea Jackson

Table of Contents

Introduction

Life, what can be said of it? It is full of love, happiness, and wonder. Yet, it is full of surprises, twists, turns, and battles. These events come at various times in our lives and with varying circumstances. These events usually cause many emotions, some good, and others not so good. Daily, many are plagued with thoughts. These thoughts are a product of many different influences, and those influences, no matter the source, create impressions. Those impressions create ideas, and those ideas turn into actions. It's imperative that we set a guard over our minds and emotions. We should inventory our influences to produce the outcomes that God desires.

The current state of our world and our society alone has caused much stress and distress in the lives of people around the world. There is an overwhelming cry for deliverance, healing, and restoration. Many are finding these times to be unbearable because they are seemingly uncontrollable. This book is for those who seem to be struggling with day-to-day life or today's life. Those who feel that they are losing their grip on reality face uncertainty, those who are seemingly without hope, and those facing difficulty transitioning. It is for those who are overwhelmed by grief and may not know that they need an intervention. Your cries have been heard, and your tears have been stored. You are not alone.

When I look at the pictures painted during this global pandemic and this time of civil unrest, I am reminded that though we are different, we share many commonalities. We share a need to receive and to give love. A need for freedom and a desire to live. Yet, as I look at the news, as I scroll social media, and as I talk with people from many walks of life, the sound that is becoming even the more loud is the one of desperation, despair, and a dulling zeal for life. However, there is an answer for that which you feel. God has declared that YOU CAN LIVE! When David was experiencing many trials and tests, he wrote, *"I shall not die, but live, and declare the works of the Lord."* Psalm 118:17 David was in the midst of a crisis. Still, his declaration matched his promise and not the reality that promoted his present.

Say it with me, I CAN LIVE, I CAN LIVE, I WILL LIVE!!! I WILL LIVE THROUGH THIS!!!! Though it may look like you're going to die, though it may look like you can't survive this crisis, though it may feel like you won't make it, YOU CAN LIVE!

CHAPTER 1

CRISIS OR CRY-SIS

What is a crisis? I am convinced that Webster, the Hebrews, the Greeks, or whoever created the word crisis misspelled its name. It should really be spelled, Cry-Sis. I am sure of it! It seemed that every time I found myself in some form of crisis, I found myself crying. I found myself sitting on my bed, sitting in my chair, or wherever I may have been. Sometimes, crying out to God and other times crying because of lack of control.

The truth is a crisis is painful. A crisis is cruel, but when in crisis, please do not break the rules. I know you must be asking, what are the rules?

THE RULES

1. **Do not Panic**
2. **Do not allow trauma to speak**

3. **You do not have to always be strong**
4. **Do not faint**

Do Not Panic

The first rule is, do not panic. I say this because it is a natural reaction. When something happens outside of our control, the fight or flight response activates, and many panic. The enemy's goal is to cause you to panic during times when productivity matters the most. You see, it's difficult to panic and be productive at the same time. Make this declaration over yourself, "I will not panic nor will I experience ungodly pressure. I will be patient and productive in every area of my life, even in crisis, in Jesus' name. Amen!"

Do Not Allow Trauma To Speak

You can not trust your trauma. It is riddled with pain, false expectations, and brokenness. It is dangerous to speak from trauma at any time but especially in times of crisis. Trauma speaks but as you are reading this, make this declaration over yourself: "I declare that I am free from trauma and every form of trauma or traumatic event in my past or present be healed in Jesus name. I declare that I will not speak from my trauma even when things appear the same. I will speak from the treasure on the inside of me, that is the Holy Spirit."

You do not have to always be strong

You do not have to be the strong one all the time. You have someone, God. He is calling you to himself, saying, cast your burdens on me. Cast the pain, the hurt, and the shame. Lean on God and your support system for strength. It is okay to feel weak sometimes.

Do Not Faint

David said he would have fainted unless he believed he would see the goodness of the Lord in the land of the living(See Psalms 27). The reality is, there is so much when dealing with a crisis in the world that could cause us to faint, but we have belief in God's plans, and that causes us to fight and endure! The crisis comes to stifle your belief, and without belief, faith falls to your feet. You were never meant to walk on faith. You were created to walk IN it! Do not allow your faith to be trampled.

CHAPTER 2

TYPES OF CRISIS

Have you ever heard the saying, "if you've seen one, you've seen them all?" This couldn't be further from the truth. Every crisis is different, and every crisis has a different effect on those involved. Most of us have faced a crisis at some point in our lives, if not all of us. Perhaps, you are involved in or facing one right now. If you or someone you know, identifying the type of crisis you're facing can help you better identify the necessary tools for survival. For purposes of this book, we will only discuss 6 of the most common types of crisis.

6 Types of Crisis

1. Identity Crisis
2. Health Crisis
3. Mental/Emotional Crisis
4. Financial Crisis

5. Loss
6. Crisis of Faith

Identity

The identity crisis is one of the biggest crises today. If you take a moment and look at the news, walk down your street, at the job, in the home, or in the church, you will see many searching for truth. Sadly, many are seeking validation from others instead of looking to God. What is an identity crisis? It is a period when one does not know who they are. There is usually an internal conflict. This type of crisis is running rampant in the culture today. Television ads, music producers, financial gurus, scientists, etc., are attempting to give definitions to and set standards that have already been given. These outlets are always telling the viewing audience what is acceptable. Often, when one does not fit the mold, they are not accepted. This lack of acceptance leads to rejection. Thus, many are searching for their spiritual fingerprint with a natural scanner.

Paul is a perfect example of one who experienced an identity crisis. For years, he was solid in his learned identity. He learned the law and the customs and assimilated well. For years he walked around full of knowledge from the Torah but couldn't find himself in it. I like to call it the Paul Identity Syndrome or P.I.S. The P.I.S. syndrome asserts that knowledge alone does not produce solid identity. It is knowledge plus encounter that produces solid identity. This means that one can attend every seminar on identity and/or listen to every sermon but be void of identity.

Is this you? Maybe you have believed you were one thing for so long, and then an encounter caused a shift in your paradigm. Now you are wondering where to go from here. Maybe your identity was found in your job, title, income, spouse, etc. Today, I challenge you to search the scriptures for who God says you are and then pray for an encounter. Knowledge plus encounter brings forth true identity.

Health

This crisis occurs when one receives an unexpected medical diagnosis. I have spoken with and consulted with many individuals who received the devastating diagnosis that challenged their faith and seemed to change their plans for their lives. Yet, these diagnoses never changed God's plan for them. In 2015, my family experienced a health crisis. My husband was at work one day when suddenly he fainted. He was taken to the emergency room, where he received a devastating report. This diagnosis was completely unexpected for a 37-year-old who was previously in perfect health. During this time, we had to constantly remind ourselves that God is a healer. I remember reading the story about Jarius's daughter in Mark 5: 21-43. Jesus not only healed the little girl, but he also raised her from the dead. This account shows the power of our God. Jarius was convinced through faith, and I am sure the testimonies of others, that Jesus could heal his daughter. He is still healing the sick today.

What health diagnosis have you or your loved one received that has caused a crisis in your life? God is bigger than every diagnosis. He is bigger than cancer, diabetes, congestive heart failure, renal disease, rheumatoid arthritis, bronchitis, high blood pressure, H.I.V./Aids, COVID-19, and any other sickness or disease.

Health Crisis prayer starter:

God our Father, thank you for this opportunity to come before you and to pray. I come to you acknowledging your greatness, your sovereignty, and your goodness. I come bringing all my cares to you because I know you care for me. Lord, the doctors have given me and/or my loved one a medical diagnosis that has caused a crisis. I know you are Lord over every crisis. Today, I declare the name of Jesus over (insert diagnosis here), and I declare my healing by the stripes of Jesus. Lord, I declare that today, I/they break free from this crisis and that healing manifests immediately in Jesus' name, Amen.

Emotional

This type of crisis usually occurs in tandem with another crisis. It can present itself in many forms. It can present as anxiety, depression, anger, and even suicidal thoughts. When we are in an emotional crisis, there are usually signs that speak to an emotional unbalance. Note, these signs do not necessarily mean the person has a long-term mental illness or chemical imbalance. However, if you or others around you have thoughts of hurting yourself or others, and/or you/they feel that a mental health evaluation by a licensed psychiatrist is needed, please consider it. Your life is valuable, and your contribution is needed.

There was a period when my family was experiencing one crisis after another. It seemed that I was coping well. At least, I thought I was. I began to suffer from situational depression. I was completing tasks, but emotionally I was detached. For me, depression did not look like sitting in a dark room, crying with my head down. For me, it was the need to keep moving, keep doing but do not feel. For me, I knew that if I allowed all the emotions in, I would lose control, and I could not afford to lose control. I stopped praying because when I talked to God, everything would pour out. I thought, now is not the time to be vulnerable. Then one day, during this season, I was tired of not feeling. During prayer, I had a fresh encounter with the Holy Spirit. I did not know that by blocking my feelings, by blocking my emotions, I was also blocking the comfort of the Holy Spirit. Survival mode will cause you to shut out an asset, the Holy Spirit. My fresh encounter with the Holy Spirit came because I chose to release.

I chose to feel, and I chose to heal. For me, it was not just telling the Holy Spirit about my pain; it was opening the door, giving him access. When you give him access, he comes in and puts things in order. Do you feel closed off emotionally? Has survival mode caused you to shut out the Holy Spirit? To stop praying? Or reduce your prayer life? Some of these signs can mean that there is a situation that sparked an emotional response. It is okay to feel and release. It is important to understand that God created us with emotions. These emotions help us experience the joys of life and the lows, but we live. He has charged us to be good stewards over what he has given us, including our emotions. We must steward our emotions well. This stewardship comes first by yielding ourselves to the Holy Spirit.

As stated, an emotional crisis can present in many ways; here are some of the other signs:

- *Changes in one's actions, i.e., moody, snappy*
- *Self-isolation (separating from loved ones, family, friends, etc.)*
- *If married (decreased or diminished desire for intimacy)*
- *Feeling "numb" or detached from situations*

Give your emotions to God. Allow the Holy Spirit to navigate the territory of your heart. Pray this with me: *Holy Spirit, I give you access to my emotions. I give you access to my pain. I repent for closing my emotions off to you. I realize that it is okay to feel, and I want to feel you(again). Help me. When I'm in survival mode, remind me that it is in you that I live, move, and have my being. Navigate the territory of my heart, mind, will, and emotions in Jesus' name.*

Financial Crisis

Financial crisis springs up when one's financial capabilities or resources cannot absorb the expenses at hand. In most cases, it starts because one cannot foot the bills and any expenses that come your way. I, too, have experienced a financial crisis. When my husband and I were married, we were relocating from another state. We had thoughts of grander concerning our move as we were going with God. We arrived in Florida and were hit with a financial crisis. We were struggling financially. We had a promise from God, a roof, law school tuition, and the necessities most times, but that was about it. We were examining our lives and living according to God's principles etc. The truth was, we were trying our best. We could not understand why God would send us to a place where we would struggle. We continued to give. We would give from what we had. Our marriage began to be impacted by the lack of finances. Suppose you are currently experiencing a financial crisis and you are married. In that case, you must guard your marriage so that this crisis does not cause a divide or feelings of resentment in your relationship. We were newlyweds, but we were battling a big giant, poverty. During this time, we saw God's supernatural power work on our behalf. Though this season was difficult, we were taught to trust God with our daily needs. God furnished our apartment; he provided food for us on days when we were not sure how we would feed our child or ourselves. This crisis taught us to depend on Jehovah Jireh. Are you currently in or facing a financial crisis? God can provide for your needs. It is as simple as it sounds, though it does not feel that simple. Will you trust God to be Jireh? I am reminded of John's declaration, "I wish above all things that you would prosper and be in good health, even as your soul prospers." As you continue to prosper in your soul, the same God that prospers your soul will prosper you financially at the level of His sufficiency for you. Make these declarations over yourself:

-I declare that as I give freely, I gain even more. I declare that because I am generous, I will prosper, and because I refresh others, I will be refreshed. ~Proverbs 11:24-25

- I declare that because I can and have been entrusted with little, I can now be entrusted with more. ~Luke 16:10

- I declare I will not wear myself out and do not trust my own cleverness. I trust God, and it is He who gives wealth. ~Proverbs 23:4

- I declare that I am a good steward over all that God gives me. I declare that my money and resources has intended purposes.

It is important to note that declarations are important, and so is stewardship. Declarations are dead without dedication and discipline. There are many reasons why we may face a financial crisis. Some reasons are in our control, while others are outside of our control. Following God's principles and addressing the things in our control is important. If you have been a poor steward(we all have at one point or another) of your financial resources, you can repent today and move forward.

Father, I repent of poor financial stewardship. I repent for not addressing the areas in my life that bring financial crisis. Lord, cause me to live a life of good stewardship and prosperity. Give me creative inventions and witty ideas to make wealth that will fund the kingdom and provide financial security in you for my house. I pray that the poverty mindset is broken off me, my family, and all future generations. We will live in the perpetual overflow of wealth and resources in Jesus' name.

Loss

Loss in and of itself can cause a crisis. Loss means being without a meaningful relationship. That relationship may be a friendship, a familial relationship, a work relationship, a spiritual relationship, or an intimate relationship. Loss of a relationship is frequently classified as emotional trauma. Still, more importantly, it is a painful loss of a particular aspect of one's life. This loss can be internal, like a loss of a good sense of self or a loss of a feeling of control over one's world, or it can even be external, like a loss of a close relationship. No matter the type of loss, it must be acknowledged and dealt with if someone wants to move on. The first step in doing so is recognizing the pain that is experienced and acknowledging it. This is done through mourning the loss. Have you lost something recently? Have you lost a job, a friendship, a relationship, a spiritual relationship? All loss is not bad, but all loss is painful.

When dealing with loss, we go through changes during the grieving process. Loss is not an uncommon occurrence, neither is it impossible to grieve. If you are going through a major loss, you may feel overwhelmed by all types of emotions, including the negative ones.

Prayer and fasting are good tools for dealing with and overcoming loss. In times of loss, I have found that gaining God's perspective helps to change mine. Though the loss is still painful, it is palatable. I know what you are thinking. How can a loss or a big loss be palatable? The loss becomes acceptable, not pleasurable. Acceptance is an important part of healing. Accepting God's will, accepting that the relationship/friendship, etc., has ended, begins the process of healing. Memories can also be a salve to lose. When we can cherish the good memories.

Some people find that going to counseling, therapy, or even talking with someone knowledgeable in this area will help them better understand their emotions and perhaps give them a better perspective for handling the situation.

Everyone will experience some kind of loss at some point in time. However, not everyone will cope with the loss in the same way. This is why we must allow the Holy Spirit to help us process and grieve the loss. There is no correct way to grieve a loss. There are different stages of loss and different degrees. In some cases, the feelings are mild, easily forgotten, slowly building, and extremely difficult to handle. Some people may experience a big change, while others may experience only a small change.

When you experience loss, you must focus on understanding the loss. Note, contrary to popular belief, there is no way to be prepared for a loss. Simulating a loss does not have the same impact as the actual loss. In times of loss, you might fail but trust in God who will not fail as He makes all perfect in His timing.

"My flesh and my heart may fail,

But God is the strength of my heart and my portion forever". - Psalm 73:26

You must address the sadness connected to the loss. There is a normal amount of sadness that follows loss. This is normal, and it can be a good thing. However, overwhelming sadness or grief should be addressed, as discussed earlier, via prayer, fasting, and seeing a Christian counselor. These tools can help the bereavement process.

Crisis Of Faith

Sadly, this type of crisis happens more frequently than one would imagine. Faith is a delicate thing because it is built upon a foundation of belief and hope. Hebrews 11:1 describes faith as *"the assurance of things hoped for, the conviction of things not seen."* When we experience tests and trials, it has a way of shaking our faith. Remember, faith is believing something that is not visible to us. A crisis of faith can happen in any area of life. Let's examine some common crisis of faith areas.

1. **Marriage/Spouse**- Many experience a crisis of faith in their marriage. It looks like loss of assurance in the "happily ever after," loss of trust in a spouse, loss of assurance regarding the direction/development of the marriage. Perhaps, it is a loss of faith in the spouse. The loss of belief in the love between the two. Have you ever lost faith in your spouse? In your marriage? Your marriage

can overcome the crisis of faith in each other and God who put you together. Re-establishing faith in the marriage means re-establishing hope in the marriage.

2. **Religious**- Unfortunately, I have seen it many times. Situations happen or arrive in life, and some lose their faith in God or their faith in the gospel that they preach. We see an example of this in scripture. John the Baptist had a brief crisis of faith in Matthew 11 when he begins to question if Jesus is the Messiah. John was in prison, and some of the things he heard Jesus was saying and teaching, caused him to have doubt. Sometimes, it can be hard to maintain your faith when you have been thrown in prison. Yet, the key to staying in faith is to ask God questions. Do not gasp for air. For so long, religion has taught us that we should not question God or ask him questions. This could not be further from the truth. God, like a loving father, wants us to inquire of him. He is waiting to answer our questions. We see this in our example here. John's faith was being tested, and instead of giving in...he sent

for answers to reassure him that what he believed was correct.

² Now when John had heard in prison the works of Christ, he sent two of his disciples,³ And said unto him, Art thou he that should come, or do we look for another? ⁴ Jesus answered and said unto them, Go and shew John again those things which ye do hear and see:⁵ The blind receive their sight, and the lame walk, the lepers are cleansed, and the deaf hear, the dead are raised up, and the poor have the gospel preached to them.
~Matthew 11:2-5

It does not matter what the crisis; Christ is over every crisis. When we submit ourselves and the crisis to him, he can lift our burdens and provide us a way of escape. We can escape in Him.

CHAPTER 3

Recognizing God In Crisis

Happiness is like the surface, but joy is like the depths of the sea. We must transcend to the surface to successfully identify our strength and victory. Our strength lies in God, and God is in the deep. So, to find God during a crisis, we must go deeper. However, I understand that it is easy to smile during times of crisis while being broken inside. Behind those smiles are depths of sadness. During those times, it is the most difficult to recognize or see God. Hurt, fear, and pain are like blinders. They limit our ability to see the goodness of God. In times of crisis, it is important to understand the will of God. We must see the promise and not just the present (surface). The deep is calling. Can you hear it?

As stated earlier, David was no stranger to crisis. We can see his growth and progression throughout the Psalms. One crisis after another began to strengthen his resolve. He understood that though he couldn't track God in this crisis, he could trust his track record. He writes:

Trust in Him at all times, O people;

Pour out your heart before Him;

God is a refuge for us. Selah. - Psalm 62:8

The strategy that David gives is simple, yet it can be difficult in tough times.

1. **Trust In Him**- Gesenius' Hebrew Lexicon defines "trust" as; "to set one's hope and confidence upon," "to be secure fearing nothing." It is many times translated as "confidence," "security," and "hope." This means that our confidence, our security, and our hope must be in God, not in things of the world.

2. **Pour Out Your Heart**- To pour means to spill forth, to expend, intensively to sprawl out. David is saying, we must bring forth

what is in us and present it to God. Pouring is an act of worship. It is done intentionally. It requires action on the part of the server. Have you poured out to God? Have you emptied your vat before him?

Often, we as people attempt to pour all out to men. We spill forth and intensively bare our hearts to those who cannot repair it, to those who cannot refill us. Don't get me wrong, we need people. They can assist us in many areas of growth, development but only God can fill us!

3. **God is the refuge-** This principle is vital during a crisis. According to Oxford Languages, a Refuge is defined as "something providing shelter." The shelter is a key to survival. We need adequate shelter from the elements. Naturally, there is not a one-and-done shelter. What would provide safety in a rainstorm may not provide the same security in a wind storm. Spiritually, we have a one-and-done shelter in times of storms. God is our

shelter. No element can eliminate Him. He is our refuge.

The Black Swan Effect

In a crisis, individuals can easily experience what is referred to in the secular world as the "The Black Swan" effect. We see this happening during this current time because of the pandemic. This effect is defined as an unpredictable or unforeseen event, typically one with extreme consequences. When these events come unexpectedly, this can spur one into a state of crisis. Has something happened in your life recently that happened unexpectedly and caused difficulty in your life or atmosphere? I know all too well the difficulty of dealing with unexpected or unforeseen events. One day, in March, my husband and I were talking. It was our normal conversation. We were both ill, but it wasn't too bad, or so I thought. Suddenly, my husband woke me, saying he could not breathe. A trip to the emergency room prompted a series of events, and by the next night, my husband was on a ventilator fighting for his life. We had contracted coronavirus, and it caught us completely off guard. I found myself, my family found ourselves in a health and emotional crisis. During this time, though I fought, the unexpected nature of this crisis left me with tears in my eyes, crying out to God. I needed to find shelter, I needed to find my trust, but I really needed to pour out my heart. It was something that I couldn't seem to do. Don't get me wrong, I prayed, but I didn't pour. There is a difference. Then, one day, sitting on the side of my bed, in worship, with tears rolling down my face, I begin to pour. I begin to pour my heart. I said, "God, help me. I was reminded in that moment of the psalmist's plea in Psalms 61:2, *...when my heart is overwhelmed, lead me to the rock that is higher than I.* My heart was truly overwhelmed. At that moment, I saw a vision; it was an altar with blood and water running down it. I was amazed. At that moment, I heard the Holy Spirit say, "My blood is enough." I cried more, but these were tears of joy. At that moment, I knew that though things didn't look well, all was well. In times of crisis, we must remember that all is well. Even when it doesn't feel well.

Generally, during this time, the time of crisis, 2 types of people or institutions emerge. Those who adjust and excel and those who fail because they could not adjust to sudden, swift change or because they were stuck in or refused to release an old paradigm. Paradigms are important in a crisis. If you want to live, depend on God. If you want to thrive, depend on God and ask him to examine your paradigm. Why is it important? A faulty paradigm will have you destroying what you should be dedicated to God. Instead of destroying your mind, you need to dedicate it to God. This is important because we must be people who adjust and move with God. To move with Him, we must first recognize him. When we immerse ourselves in Him, when he moves, we move. Dedicate your mind, thoughts, emotions, finances, identity, and crisis… give it all to God. In doing this, we are never stuck, surprised maybe, need time to compose ourselves, yes but never stuck. This does not negate the difficulty and the turbulence involved in the transition; it means that the wave is so powerful, it forces movement. This wave that I am speaking of is the person of the Holy Spirit. He is so powerful; he is like a mighty wave. When He moves in us, it causes us to move.

CHAPTER 4

Alone With My Thoughts

Thoughts are a powerful tool utilized by God and, at times, can be utilized by the enemy. They can be an ally or foe. This is particularly the case when we face difficult situations. These thoughts can be a blessing or a curse. There were times in my life, when in crisis, that I questioned a lot of things. These thoughts seemed to surface more when I was alone. What thoughts do you have when you are alone?

As a believer, we must be fully present with our thoughts, especially when we are alone. When the enemy tries to make subtle suggestions that mimic the truth with a little lie mixed in. Therefore, we must guard our minds. Paul tells the believers in Corinth that our thoughts can run away from us. He asserts that we must bring every thought captive to the obedience of Christ.

"Casting down imaginations, and every high thing that exalteth itself against the knowledge of God, and bringing into captivity every thought to the obedience of Christ;" ~ 2 Corinthians 10:5

Why are thoughts so important? Thoughts that linger become actions. Every great victory or defeat started in mind. This is evident even from the foundation of the world. God said, "let us make man in our image…" Man was a thought before he was a created being. What have you created in your thoughts that has manifested into your reality?

[26] And God said, Let us make man in our image, after our likeness: and let them have dominion over the fish of the sea, and over the fowl of the air, and over the cattle, and overall the earth, and over every creeping thing that creepeth upon the earth. ~ Genesis 1:26

When in crisis, take a moment of silence and listen to your thoughts. This way, you know what thoughts and strongholds you need to pull down.

Crisis causes thoughts to run through your mind in rapid-fire succession.

Ways to manage your thoughts:

Prayer- Releasing our thoughts to God and asking the Holy Spirit to help us change our thought patterns or retrain our thoughts will help mitigate negative thoughts.

Reading- Reading can be a great way to replace negative thoughts. Reading God's words and what he has to say concerning you and your situation can be beneficial in identifying the lies of the enemy. When we recognize a lie, we can refute the lie. Often, in crisis, the enemy takes advantage of the fact that we are so focused on the crisis, not his tactics.

Another tactic that the enemy uses is a distraction. It is easy to become distracted from purpose when you are in the midst of a crisis and are alone with your thoughts. Thinking about certain things distracts you from the work that you are really supposed to be doing. This can cause you to procrastinate. The key here is not to think about the crisis but to think about Christ.

Focus on the good things. Paul tells the believers in Philippi to shift their thoughts.

"Finally, brethren, whatsoever things are true, whatsoever things are honest, whatsoever things are just, whatsoever things are pure, whatsoever things are lovely, whatsoever things are of good report; if there be any virtue, and if there be any praise, think on these things." ~Philippians 4:8

Paul is giving the church things to think about. This is what we must do. Occupy our minds with the truth, with praise, and good reports.

When you are alone with your thoughts in prayer, remember that God wants you to be in joy. God gives us control of our thoughts. We control what dominates them.

When we understand that we have the power to give our thoughts over to the Holy Spirit and to rule and govern them, it shifts our alone time. We don't have to be afraid of our thoughts because we have the power to pull down strongholds and change our thoughts to Godly ones.

Remember that there is hope. Your thoughts are powerful. You can turn even the most critical times of your life into an opportunity for growth. There is nothing you cannot accomplish when you filter your mind. So, when you are alone with your thoughts, keep those thoughts positive, and you will find hope. This is one reason for prayer - to help you keep a positive attitude obtained through positive interactions with God. It doesn't matter what circumstances you may be in.

"Draw nigh to God, and he will draw nigh to you. Cleanse [your] hands, [ye] sinners; and purify [your] hearts, [ye] double minded". - James 4:8

The bottom line is that you can handle whatever comes your way when you have the right mindset. Some people find it difficult to change their thinking when they are in life's situations. If you are one of these people, remember that it will get easier as you go along the road to becoming mentally stronger.

When you are at the end of your road, do not be afraid to look back and look at all you have achieved with the Holy Spirit. Your journey has only just begun. You have power and strength in you that will carry you into many more amazing seasons in your life.

CHAPTER 5

The "D" & "S" Words

The elephants in the room are sounding loud but no one sees them. Unfortunately, depression and suicide are words that are considered taboo in the life of believers. As a believer, you should say that you are great, you love the Lord, and all is well. I am all for, and I believe strongly in the power of confession. However, religion has taught so many to mask the pain instead of treating it. It is as such; I want you to be free but not around me. This is a topic I know well. Many feel ashamed of thoughts of depression and suicide because I am a Christian. The reality is depression and suicide can affect our fleshly bodies just as any other aliment. If you are currently facing one of these monsters, know that Jesus never meant for these things to be put under the rug but rather under the blood. Depression, even though it does not feel good, is something that one can overcome. This is especially true in the life of a Christian because we have faith in God, who will heal even the deepest darkest places in our lives. Scripture tells us that knowledge is essential to survival. We see this in Hosea 4:6:

"My people are destroyed for lack of knowledge: because thou hast rejected knowledge, I will also reject thee, that thou shalt be no priest to me: seeing thou hast forgotten the law of thy God, I will also forget thy children."

Knowledge brings freedom and deliverance. Therefore, understanding what depression looks like and its cause can make for more targeted prayers and fasting. Situational depression is just the result, but it is not the root of the problem. Get to the root, and the result of it leaves.

Depression is a profoundly serious condition. What causes situational depression? Crisis. It can result from stress at work, death, illness, loss of a loved one, loss of a meaningful relationship, etc. In severe cases, it can produce physical symptoms such as tremors, sweating, hot flashes, headaches, dizziness, nausea, diarrhea, etc.

There are times when a person is not aware of what is happening. As I stated previously, I was dealing with situational depression, and I did not recognize it. It manifested as difficulty sleeping, going to the restroom often, and unable to remember things in some cases. These are all signs that there is a problem and that you should dig. It may not be the underlying cause, but a professional should be consulted.

Situational depression often changes as the situation changes. Yet, depending on the seriousness of the situation, it may be best to see a doctor or immediately seek professional help if symptoms become overbearing. As soon as you notice increasing symptoms, it is best to address them.

Sometimes, this form of depression has a serious effect on a person's life. For instance, if there is a loss of a loved one, a traumatic event may have occurred, making it difficult to grieve. This type of depression can also affect a career-oriented person. If the person lost a job or had a serious accident that was not in their control, situational depression may occur. You can shake that feeling of worthlessness, uselessness, and hopelessness.

When depression is present in a person's life for any length of time, it can negatively impact their life. This depression, when not identified and addressed, opens the door to suicidal thoughts or the act itself.

Suicide

Suicidal thoughts are at an all-time high. Some in the body battle this monster, but few people talk about it. It is another elephant in the room. A person privately struggling with suicidal thoughts usually has a history of unhealed trauma. Trauma, when left unhealed, leads to depression and sometimes suicidal thoughts. However, today, if you are reading this and feel that you cannot expose these suicidal thoughts, know that there is help for you. It does not matter who you are. Know that you do not have to fight alone or in silence. There are many people ready and willing to fight with and for you. You can overcome this giant. Most importantly, know that God is near you.

"The Lord is near to the brokenhearted and saves the crushed in spirit." ~Psalm 34:18

It's a trick

Satan is the master of tricks, and he is the master of mind games. As I stated earlier, he implants thoughts in minds to make one believe they are alone, that no one understands them, or convinces them that leaving the world is the only way to stop the pain. All of these are fallacies. Life was never designed to consist of unbearable pain. You were created with purpose, and to fulfill that purpose, you must live. Honestly, the pain will come, but the pain will also pass when given an exit or an outlet. The enemy wants you to believe that you need to make an exit when actually it is the pain that needs to leave.

Have you given your pain an outlet? Have you identified the source of the pain? Have you been vocal about your pain? Do you have a support system? A judgment-free zone? Know that not only can you run to the Father in prayer, but you can also run to others. Maybe you are saying, I've tried talking with others, but they betrayed me or judged me. While this may be true of one, it is not true of all. This is no reason to stop trying.

If you find yourself in a serious depression or suicidal situation, you should consider contacting a Christian counselor and/or joining a Christian support group as soon as possible.

Please remember that depression and suicidal thoughts can happen to anyone at any time during a crisis in their lives. Seek help. If you find yourself suffering from suicidal thoughts, you should not wait to address these thoughts. The perfect time is now. As you are reading this, let us pray. Father, wrap your arms around the person reading this. I command the spirit of death, depression, and suicide to release them, their thoughts, and come out of them now, in Jesus' name. Holy Spirit, move as only you can in my heart, my will, and my emotions. Forgive me for wanting to escape the gift of life that has been given to me. Teach me how to navigate and overcome in the land of the living. I expose every suicidal thought and feeling to you today. Now, because it is uncovered, I can breathe, and now I can live. Move, Holy Spirit, Move. I invite you to do the miraculous in me. In Jesus' name, Amen!

If you prayed this prayer, welcome to freedom. I pray that you will connect with believers who can help you maintain your freedom and deliverance.

Next Steps

1. If you are not, connect to a local church/body of believers. It is there that

you will be introduced to other iron that can sharpen you.

2. Develop a transparent prayer life. Laying out everything before God.

3. Develop an intimate relationship with the Holy Spirit. You can talk to him, just as I am talking to you.

4. Identify your support system. Those who can serve as accountability and walk this journey with you. Those with who you can be raw and transparent with.

There is help for depression and suicide, and there is hope for those who suffer, whether situational or the disease.

 Note: You can seek treatment at a medical facility or through a Christian-based treatment program. When coupled with deliverance and prayer, both options can be effective. They can give you the strength that you need to overcome depression and suicide and live again.

Do not allow depression and suicide to control your life. Even if it seems like it is the easiest thing globally, you should never ignore the warning signs. If you feel like you are drowning or are losing control, reach out again and again. It is not too late. It is better to do something about it now. You are not a burden; your heart just may be burden down. We command every burden to live, now in Jesus' name. You can live. You will live.

CHAPTER 6

OVERCOMING TRAUMA

Trauma is real, and it affects many believers. According to apa.org, trauma is defined as "an emotional response to a terrible event." However, each person can describe trauma in a unique way. It is a fluid term that can be subjective. A crisis has been known to cause trauma when proper coping skills and mechanisms are not in place. Trauma occurs because the person is unsuspecting of traumatic events. It is the result of unhealed emotions. Healing is not only for our mortal bodies, but it is also for our emotions and our thought life. Trauma can be experienced in many forms, but the form most often associated with a crisis is referred to as "Traumatic Stress." I know the effects of this very well.

Traumatic stress is feelings that initiate the fight/flight response in our bodies. Many who are faced with this type of trauma during or after a crisis experience seemingly random responses in their bodies like breathlessness, panic attacks, terror, or cloudy/ dream-like vision. It is produced when our bodies compensate or attempt to respond to the emotions we feel. I did not know that I was dealing with traumatic stress because society and the church teaches, be tough, go through, and move on. I remember the day in 2018 like yesterday. I was driving, and immediately my vision became blurred, and it seemed as though it was foggy. I visited my doctors and explained my symptoms. They ran many tests only to come to no resolve. There was not an identifiable diagnosis. I voiced my concerns to other leaders in the church, no one had an answer. At this point, I did not believe I was "stressed." I thought I was coping rather well with life and everything happening in my family. It was not easily identifiable. We tend to vilify what we cannot identify. Are you currently facing some of these systems? If you answered yes, you can and will overcome every form of trauma in your life. I declare the root of your trauma will be identified and rectified, In Jesus' name.

"For we walk by faith, not by sight." ~2 Corinthians 5:7

Overcoming trauma is a faith walk. We do the work, and we watch God work at the same time. We must ask ourselves the hard questions if we are to overcome trauma. Are you ready? Ask yourselves these questions:

1. What is the root cause of the crisis?
2. How do I feel about the circumstances surrounding the crisis?
3. How does my emotional response show up in my life?
4. Am I currently experiencing any of the systems of traumatic stress? If so, what are they?
5. What is my responsibility/role in my healing?
6. What is the Holy Spirit's role in my healing?

One of the main reasons crisis survivors or those currently in crisis experience traumatic stress is a refusal to address the crisis. This is especially true in the body of Christ because we have a "be strong" no matter what. Yes, we are too strong in the Lord. To get the strength, we must make our way to the Lord. Too often, many believers feel that they should only pray and put a Band-Aid on the wound. This covers but does not heal.

There is a stigma attached to a Christian needing healing from trauma. However, this is counter to the gospel of Jesus Christ because he came to bring healing in every area. As a deliverance minister, I can attest that identifying stigma and trauma is necessary for deliverance. Have you been or are you now bound because you are a Christian and are ashamed to say that you are experiencing these symptoms? I have experienced the shame associated with trauma-induced stress. I felt that because I was a Christian, because I was an intercessor and because I was a leader, admitting that I faced breathlessness, panic attacks made me look weak and lack faith. I remember having conversations with some other leaders. I shared my heart, and my comments were dismissed. I believe there was a genuine concern, but addressing the issue would mean a level of responsibility to assist me with the soul work. If you are currently feeling overwhelmed, it is okay to say that.

Talk to someone, declare and decree over yourself and your situation. During that time, I ran from conference to conference, hoping someone would see and "pickup" my pain and trauma. I remember thinking, I cannot live like this. I cannot live and thrive when I feel that my breathing is being restricted. I also felt guilty during this time. Guilt will keep you bound. I remember thinking, I would not be dealing with this if I prayed more. I need to pray more. This was my resolve. While this was great and deliverance occurred, the Holy Spirit addressed my spiritual need. Systems and boundaries needed to be put in place. Support systems needed to re-established.

It is okay to re-establish healthy boundaries. Seasons change and look different than others. The boundaries set for your last season or the last crisis may not work this time. I was charged to do the natural work. May I add that prayer is always good!

Do not beat yourself up. God comes to help you, not lock you into a mental prison of guilt. During this time, I administered self-deliverance, thinking that it was some type of demonic oppression. Yet, I never addressed the root or the beginning of the trauma. Everything you face is not a demon. Sometimes you need to learn new patterns and learn coping skills. If you want to overcome trauma, you must identify its cause, address unhealthy patterns and create healthy patterns. I am sharing this testimony because you may be reading this thinking; I am in that place. I need help; I feel like I cannot breathe. Know that you do not have to walk through this situation alone. Healing is your portion, and you can overcome trauma. You were created to conquer. You are resilient. Resilience is our ability to bounce back from difficult situations. Resilience does not mean that one is excused from any negative effects of the crisis, only that one has the necessary skills to live. It is time for you to bounce back! It is time for you to live. Here are some ways you can bounce back:

1. Find meaning in the crisis. Look for the positive.
2. Identify the positive relationships in your life and connect. (If you do not have positive relationships in your life, support

groups can be beneficial) You were never meant to do this alone.

3. Identify strengths and ways to improve perceived weaknesses.

CHAPTER 7

How Did I Get Here?

Crisis has a way of causing us to ask the question, "How Did I get here?" This is because people tend to disconnect themselves to mask the pain of the trauma. Then at the end of the crisis, one finds themselves in unfamiliar territory, a foreign land. Questioning and taking inventory in our lives as Christians is important. Many scriptures encourage self-examination. Paul frequents the topic in his letters.

"Examine yourselves, whether ye be in the faith; prove your own selves. Know ye, not your own selves, how that Jesus Christ is in you, except yet be reprobates?" ~2Corinthians 13:5

Examination during and after a crisis is important. It allows one to inventory faith. A crisis is used by God to increase our faith and dependency on Him. No, he does not cause the trials, but he does allow them. Jesus warned us that there would be a time of tribulation, there would be a rise in evil and oppression, and there would be persecutions.

"Knowing this, that the trying of your faith worketh patience." ~James 1:3

Trials can seem endless. During one of the most trying times in my walk, the crisis seemed perpetual. I found myself asking God, "How long will I be in this place?" I was hurting, broken, and tired. Until one day, I looked up, and I had not prayed in over two weeks. I believe that my patience wore thin, and I conceded in battle. I believed that he was with me, but I did not understand how he would allow me to be in that place.

Everyone has a "How did I get here?" moment, though not all will admit it. For me, It was during a time in my life where I had been challenged emotionally and spiritually by the demands of serving others. I remember being invited into a non-denominational church, having my faith questioned, and finding the courage to stand up and speak out. While I didn't know quite what to make of it all, I soon began to understand what the call of duty and faith meant. It is so important for each of us to take responsibility for our own actions, to claim our accountability for our life and love, and to work hard to move beyond the limitations of our current state. If we do not, then we will never move beyond the boundaries of our current state.

When we are in a state of ignorance about God, about the crisis, and about our lives, it usually means that we have forgotten Him somehow and have become focused on our problems and difficulties. He wants us to be moved beyond this state of limitation. Because of His teachings, He has us prepared to be the vessels that enter and exit the promises of God. Maneuvering through difficult places with peace and patience. Crisis Overcoming crisis requires full surrender to the Holy Spirit. He is our guide through this life. However, if we chose to occupy the status of spectators, waiting but not being willing for His presence to purify us, so we can get healed, then we have already bought into the very thing that we are fighting against, stagnation, and that is not living.

The crisis has a way of addressing the issues of complacency and dependency. Where or with whom does your dependence lie? Do not act in haste, in fear, without a solid foundation, and in a state of doubt and confusion.

During a crisis, it is easy to limit the Holy Spirit. Be careful not to ignore the voice of God.

CHAPTER 8

The Art Of Resting

The art of resting and having faith in God for breakthroughs is vital at every point in our lives but especially during a crisis. To sit before God and worship Him and give all your cares to Him is an oasis in the desert. I frequently recount the lesson and instruction that I was given by the Holy Spirit during a time of great difficulty. I was in a physical and emotional crisis. My body was reacting and responding to everything happening around and within me. As Calvin and I cried out in prayer, my prayer began to shift, and I felt an overwhelming cry. I began to weep in God's presence. Though I did not vocalize that I was tired at this moment, the Father knew. The depths of my heart were speaking to him. Have you allowed the depths of your heart to speak to Him? My heart was speaking, and God's response spoke to the deep place in me. The Holy Spirit said, "rest in my bosom." To hear those words brought me to tears even more. The Father was giving me permission to rest. Though I was in the middle of the crisis, he said it is okay to rest because you are surrounded by me. Rest is a beautiful thing. I know that you may feel tired. You can take a rest in him.

"Come unto me, all ye that labour and are heavy laden, and I will give you rest. Take my yoke upon you, and learn of me; for I am meek and lowly in heart: and ye shall find rest unto your souls." ~Matthew 11:28-29

Resting is an act of warfare. I am waging war by trusting my Father. I am waging war by believing that Christ is over every crisis.

Rest, knowing that there is no such thing as living a perfect life. We all have problems; we all may face a crisis, some more severe than others. If we can accept this fact, rest becomes easier, and we are free to approach God and speak to Him about the issues in our lives.

Some people choose to avoid God in crisis. This is an error. Rather, run to Him, rest in Him, abide in Him.

The art of resting and having faith in God for a breakthrough comes when we are willing to surrender and rest. Many who have followed Jesus have gone through rough times, so you are not alone. The key is to not fall away. Stand and rest. Remain consistent in all that he has spoken. Why? Because the road to wholeness and finding peace and happiness lies in our ability to rest while God is working through our problems.

Rest does not mean that you will be free of pain. You may still encounter frustration and disappointment. It may involve uncertainty, and at times tears are shed along with anger and frustration, but the key is knowing that you are safe in his bosom.

CHAPTER 9

Where Do I Go From Here?

"These things I have spoken unto you, that in me ye might have peace. In the world ye shall have tribulation: but be of good cheer; I have overcome the world." - John 16:33

The journey through life is filled with trials and tribulations. Though they may be unavoidable, we can overcome hard times with Christ. We can overcome it when we put our trust in him because He has already overcome the world.

When overcoming hard times and confusion as a Christian, we must try to identify the cause of the troubles first and then find a solution to your problems.

Secondly, we should be willing to sacrifice for our salvation. Hard times are inevitable but we can definitely traverse them with Christ. One key is learning to live with and cooperate with the Holy Spirit daily, not just in times of crisis. A lot of Christians today are quick to take refuge in God when they have faced trouble but run away from Him when the clouds have cleared. They justify their actions by saying that it was God's plan all along to guide them and teach them in their time of need. This is true but he also wants to guide us everyday. Truth is, we always need God, no matter the season. God is the one guiding us and will guide us but we must have an ear to hear Him.

So, how do you overcome hard times and confusion as a Christian? Surrender to God and surrender to His will. Sometimes, we find ourselves fighting against the will of God and it makes tough seasons more difficult. The Bible teaches us to resist the devil and he will flee. The same is for our flesh, if we resist it, it will be subdued.

It may seem like an obvious thing to say, but too many Christians fall into the trap of expecting God to take care of everything when we have been given a responsibility as well. The Bible says that we are to humble ourselves before Him. This means that we should expect God to protect and provide for us and be generous with His resources. Asking how to overcome hard times and confusion as a Christian means that we should become more appreciative of what God has already done for us, knowing that what lies before us can be conquered with Him.

"I pray that the eyes of your heart will have enough light to see what is the hope of God's call, what is the richness of God's glorious inheritance among believers." — Ephesians 1:18

We can overcome any crisis we learn to humble ourselves, walk in humility, walk with the Holy Spirit. The journey from here on must be one of faith. You must learn to walk by faith. God must be your first answer and not our last resource. Trust that whatever situation comes your way, He can help you get through it.

When you were a child, did you have any doubt about where you were going or who would make it happen? Most would answer No. Children trust that their parents or guardians will provide for them, care for them and love them. Turn that fear into a child-like dependance on God. Life moves so quickly, so enjoy God, enjoy those in your circle and love hard.

Though there may be difficilities that lie ahead, know that you will survive.

CONCLUSION

You can live through a crisis. It requires self-examination, submission to God, and being willing to sacrifice. I have found that many believers are willing to make some sacrifices but are often unwilling to ask God or others for help when things get tough. Society has created a self-sufficient body rather than one dependent upon God and community. It is heartbreaking, and the reason so many give up instead of giving in to God.

To survive a crisis, the first step is to identify the cause of the crisis, submit to God, then develop a Godly support system.

When Jesus Christ became incarnated and began His mission on this earth, he came with a promise that those who would believe would be saved and have eternal life. Yet, our faith takes us further. Because we have delegated power and authority, we can rise above the world and circumstances in the world because of Jesus' perfect obedience to the will of God.

Will crisis come? Yes. Will Christ triumph over and in every crisis? Yes. We must be sure to examine our hearts in crisis that we do not hit the two extremes. We do not become prideful or fall away from the faith. Pride has caused much havoc in believers due to the, "I can do this by myself." It causes believers to suffer in silence, but you do not have to suffer alone. Others fall away from the faith and become enlightened in other areas because they feel that God deserted them and left them dying. However, this is a trick from the enemy. God will never leave us nor forsake us.

"Let your conversation be without covetousness; and be content with such things as ye have: for he hath said, I will never leave thee, nor forsake thee." ~Hebrews 13:5

Believers know that God is bigger than all problems. There is hope for you if you have lost everything, lost finances, lost jobs, lost marriages lost loved ones, lost friends, even to the point of death. There is no reason to give up on life or the God of your salvation. The only way is total dependence upon Him. Stop worrying about what it looks like, what others may say, and focus on God.

I CAN LIVE